THE GIFT OF CHRISTMAS

THE GIFT OF CHRISTMAS:

A Closer Look

E. L. C. Austin

BAKER BOOK HOUSE
Grand Rapids, Michigan

PHOTOLITHOPRINTED BY CUSHING - MALLOY, INC.
ANN ARBOR, MICHIGAN, UNITED STATES OF AMERICA

To Bernie
whose persistent insistence
and patient prodding
got the book written

Preface

The Gift of Christmas is an attempt to set forth, as briefly as possible, the historical, scriptural, astronomical, biographical, and geographical facts necessary for a clear comprehension of this most momentous event of human history.

Because of the story's tremendous importance and great human appeal, myths and legends have so encrusted the historic event that the truth is often obscured by fables. But the real story is far more fascinating than any of its embellishments.

Contents

PART ONE
The Quiet Girl

A Visitor
from Outer Space

The astonishing and dramatic story of the birth of the Lord Jesus Christ really has no beginning that can be reckoned in human time, for He had no beginning. But the story has to start somewhere for us, and Dr. Luke starts the story here:

> There was in the days of Herod, the king of Judea, a certain priest named Zacharias... and his wife was of the daughters of Aaron, and her name was *Elisabeth*. Luke 1:5.

The Old King

Here are our first three characters, and what an astonishing contrast they are. This Herod was the one that Flavius Josephus called "the Great." Josephus is our source for the life and times of Herod, and he may have given him this grand title in genuine admiration of Herod's quite extraordinary gifts of administration. Or it could have been an acknowledgment of the Emperor's opinion, for Josephus quotes Caesar and Agrippa as saying, "The dominions of Herod were too little for the greatness of his soul." Or, Josephus may have used that title to distinguish him from the many "Herods" who came after him. Herod's political acumen was demonstrated by the fact that he managed, for nearly thirty-four years, to rule a people who hated him, and to maintain the friendship of Rome during years of shifting intrigue and treacheries.[1]

As a young man he had been a man of remarkable vigor, initiative, and cunning. He was a great builder who imported artisans and architects from Italy and rebuilt Jerusalem in the image of Rome.

The modern state of Israel has built a marvelous miniature model of ancient Jerusalem that covers 2,500 square feet. Every little building is made of small, hand-cut stones. It is curious to note that the Israelis did not reproduce David's Jerusalem or the magnificence of Solomon's Jerusalem; they rebuilt Herod's Jerusalem. The Jews never had a more hated ruler or one who deserved that hatred more. Nevertheless, their city attained its greatest magnificence under Herod the Great and the despised Romans. (It must be mentioned in all honesty that another factor is the meager records still existing of what Solomon's rich capital looked like. The Roman records are plentiful and a thousand years closer. And, of course, the great majority of the tourists from the western world are at least nominally Christian and want to see the Jerusalem "where Jesus walked.")

This Herod was the one who built the mountain fortress of Masada, that castle in the sky, and the best aqueducts Jerusalem ever had. But Herod was not a Jew and had no business ruling in the city of David. He was an Idumean, that is, a descendant of Esau. He was what we call today an Arab, and you can imagine what modern Israel would think if the United Nations appointed an able, but unscrupulous Arab prince as mayor of Jerusalem. Rome had chosen

Herod, who served Rome well and was a treacherous "friend" of Antony and Cleopatra.

At the time of our story he was an old man and insanely murderous. He had killed three of his many sons and seven other close relatives, for he feared they were plotting to take his crown. In an Othello-like plot he had killed his beautiful Jewish queen, Marianne (who was one of ten wives) because he had been told by palace intriguers that she was disloyal to him. He lived in daily, consuming fear that someone, somehow, would wrench the kingdom away from him.

In Herod's city was the temple Herod built for the Jews. They paid for it with exorbitant taxes, and they loved it with extravagant pride. The temple complex contained, in addition to the sanctuary, libraries, storerooms, the Sanhedrin assembly hall, and apartments for the hundreds of priests who came from their villages throughout Palestine to live and serve in the temple for three months of each year. Among those priests there was a man who is the second character of the great drama.

The Old Priest

The second person mentioned in Luke 1:5 is the old priest Zacharias, and it is impossible to imagine who could be more of a contrast to Herod. Luke characterizes him as righteous, blameless, childless, and old.

On this certain sabbath the temple was the place a momentous event was being prepared, but not by the Jewish priests. Their type of service was determined by drawing lots, and Zacharias's turn had come to burn the incense at the hour of prayer. The sweet ascending smoke of the burning frankincense was the visible representation of the prayers of Israel. But the prayers had been ascending for centuries without any response. It had been nearly 450 years

since God had made His last statement to Israel in Malachi,
and not one word since: no visions, no dreams, no mes-
sages, no miracles. Four centuries is a long time in human
history. (For us it would be like not receiving a divine message since the time of Columbus.) In all those years God
had not acknowledged His chosen people. They had been
destroyed by the Babylonians and Assyrians, occupied and
ruled by the Medes and the Persians, the Greeks and the
Romans.

Gabriel Arrives

On this particular day Zacharias was doing what he had
doubtless done hundreds of times in his life but as he stood
before the smoking altar with outstretched arms, he suddenly realized that he was not alone in the Holy Place. On
his right stood a Man in luminous clothing. The golden altar
of incense was approximately eighteen inches square. If
Zacharias stood in front of the altar, and the Visitor stood at
the right side of it, they would have been within arm's reach
of each other.

This person that Zacharias saw should be explained, for I
think that it is he who appears in the story no less than seven
times. He is only named four times in the entire Bible, and
in three of those instances his name appears only
incidentally—almost by accident. He is named when he is
dispatched to Mary, but he does not tell her his name. Here,
in this appearance to Zacharias, he is simply called by his
title, the angel of the Lord, until Zacharias expresses in-
credulity at the message. Then he responds (a little indig-
nantly, I think), "I am Gabriel. I stand in the presence of
God." The implied question is, Would a person in such a
position lie?

In the Book of Daniel, he is not named, but Daniel over-
hears a Voice addressing him as "Gabriel," and giving him

instructions about what to tell Daniel. In Daniel 9 Daniel mentions that the "Gabriel" whom he had previously seen came to him again.

We have some very good descriptions of Gabriel. Daniel writes (in chaps. 8 and 9) that he has the appearance of a man, not a winged creature. There is an order of angels that is called the *Bene Elohim,* that is, "sons of God," mentioned in Job 1:6; 2:1; 38:7. This is the highest honor God can bestow upon a created being (I John 3:1). The words *Bene Elohim* mean, among other things, that the angels were created in the image of God, the pre-incarnate Lord Jesus Christ, who walked with Adam in the garden, wrestled with Jacob at the brook, and talked with Moses face to face on Sinai. Since both angels and man were created in this same image, they look like us. The angel of the Lord appeared to Cornelius, the Roman centurion, who described him to Peter as "a man in bright clothing." Mark (16:5) and Luke (24:4) describe the angels at the garden tomb as young men in bright clothing.

In the case of the nativity, Gabriel seems to have been from this very first appearance to Zacharias, the angel in charge of arrangements. On four occasions, someone called "the angel of the Lord" appeared to Joseph in dreams with instructions about how to protect the child. (God communicated with both the Old Testament Joseph and the New Testament Joseph by dreams.) The angel of the Lord was the one sent to Bethlehem with the good tidings of great joy. I can't imagine that it could have been anyone less than Gabriel, who had been so involved in this from the beginning.

Zacharias was both startled and afraid when Gabriel appeared. But the angel reassured him:

> Fear not, Zacharias: for thy prayer is heard; and thy wife Elisabeth shall bear thee a son, and thou shalt call his name John. Luke 1:13.

It must have been thirty years since Zacharias had last made that petition. What an odd thing to be told that a thirty-year-old prayer had been heard!

Zacharias's reaction and answer was perfectly natural, but unfortunate. He said:

> How do I know you are telling me the truth? This is impossible. We are both old and my wife is long past childbearing. Luke 1:18 (paraphrased).

The One in luminous clothing was angry.

> I am Gabriel. I stand in the presence of God. I was sent with this message. Would I lie to you? You will not speak another word until the child is born. Luke 1:19–20 (paraphrased).

The men waiting in the court of the Israelites for the triple blessing (Num. 6:24-26) to be pronounced began to be aware that Zacharias had been inside unusually long. There must have been a small stir and murmur as they whispered to each other about the delay. Then he came out, looking very strange. He lifted his hand to say, "The Lord bless thee and keep thee . . . ," but no words came out of his mouth. Trembling and dazed he tried to tell them with gestures what he had seen. He did finish his tour of duty and must have written an explanation to the other priests. Then he went home to Elisabeth and wrote her an account not omitting the baby's name and some weeks later she found it was all true. She was indeed pregnant.

It is rather touching to read: " . . . and she hid herself five months. . . . " The life-long reproach of barrenness had been taken away in her old age of all things! Elisabeth quotes Rachel's joyful words in Genesis 30:23, "God hath taken away my reproach." But I think she felt like Sarah, who also bore her only child in her old age. Probably the hiding was simply to wait until her pregnancy was beyond dispute, and no one would think her an addled old woman who was imagining things. I knew a woman who bore a child late in life. She tells me she just walked around the house laughing out loud to herself and singing little songs.

Zacharias means "God remembers" and Elizabeth means "the oath of God." Together they spell out the truth that God always remembers His oath, the sworn promises that He made to Abraham and to David. Zacharias and Elizabeth had for years entreated the Lord for a child, and God's answer was to give them not just an ordinary child but to wait and send them a very special child. He was, in fact, called by his cousin Jesus the greatest man ever born of woman (Matt. 11:11).

This is how God broke His long silence and this is the prelude.

A Servant Named Mary

A Town Near Armageddon

Sixty miles north of Jerusalem by air or ninety miles on the then-preferred trans-Jordan road, Nazareth lies in a little cup of hills, tipped to the south so that it overlooks the plain of Armageddon. Armageddon is also called the Valley of Jezreel and is a beautifully fertile place, perhaps because for at least fifty centuries it has been regularly fertilized with the blood and bones of warriors. The roster of generals who have fought in that green triangular valley reads like a summary of history: Pharaoh Necho, Nebuchadnezzar, Richard the Lion-Hearted, Suleiman the Magnificent, Napoleon, Lord Allenby, and General Pershing are some of the names we recognize.

Nazareth means "Branch-town" for it comes from the Hebrew word *netser* for "branch."

This derivation of the name of the town has been advanced by a number of scholars as the most likely explanation for Matthew's statement (2:23) that "he... dwelt in . . . Nazareth: that it might be fulfilled which was spoken by the prophets, He shall be called a Nazarene'' (2:23). The problem is that such a statement does not exist in this form in the Old Testament. Matthew said that prophets (plural) spoke this message, and there are two statements each by three of the prophets that there would be One who would be called "the Branch" (See Isa. 4:2, 9:14; Jer. 23:5, 33:15; and Zech. 3:8, 6:12). It is possible, and seems to me a likely solution to this scholarly problem, that when later He was referred to as "the Nazarene" it carried a reference to the Branch from Branchtown.

Under the Roman occupation Nazareth was just a small, hillbilly town, regarded by the urbanites of Decapolis and Caesarea as almost beneath notice. Their attitude was exactly like that of any inhabitant of the American eastern seaboard cities toward a mountain town in the backwoods of Tennessee or Virginia. Nazareth was an ideal location for obscurity. It is not even mentioned in the Old Testament.

> Did you say Nazareth?
> But nothing good can come
> from Nazareth.
>
> Nazareth is nowhere—
> a hillbilly village—
> the boondocks of Galilee.
>
> No one who is *anyone*
> has ever heard of it.
> Who would choose to live there?
>
> You say that men
> will hear of Nazareth?!

The Servant Girl

In this despised town, among its possibly four or five hundred inhabitants, there was a girl who must have been considered among the least in its social structure. In Luke's account, Mary twice refers to herself as the Lord's *doulē,* which means servant or bondslave. In the Old Testament, the equivalent term was used in three ways: of actual servants and purchased slaves (most often); of concubines; and by free women when referring to themselves, as a sign of courtesy and humility. This last figurative usage we find when Ruth called herself handmaid to Boaz; Hannah referred to herself by the same term; the beautiful Abigail, wife of Nabal, called herself handmaid when talking with David. The word is used fifty-one times in the Old Testament, more often literally than merely politely, for slavery was the sad fact of life. It is used of only one person in the New Testament: Mary. (There is also a New Testament quotation [Acts 2:18] of an Old Testament prophecy [Joel 2:29] about the handmaidens.) But as the late Dr. David L. Cooper, translator and master of both Hebrew and Greek often said, "When the literal sense makes sense, do not look for another sense, or insist on a figurative meaning."

The King James' translation of the word *doulē* as *handmaiden* has been followed by most other English translations. Its connotation is that it describes a lady, or at least a lady-in-waiting. It faintly echoes the gracious life of a courtly society. But Nazareth had no elegance, and in Mary's case there are several reasons to believe that she was using the word in its most literal sense. I notice that Berkeley Version does translate the word in its usual, primary meaning, and says, "servant-girl."

Mary makes four statements in her exalting song of praise, called "the Magnificat" (Luke 1:46–54), that certainly indicate a very lowly position. She mentions her "low estate" and her "low degree" and by implication classes herself with the poor and hungry. As we get acquainted with this girl, we will find that she is always very practical and realistic about life. Her appraisal of her social status must be taken at face value; very probably she was an indentured servant.[1]

The Missing Persons

As we read and reread the story in Luke 1 and 2 and in Matthew 2, we will finally notice that there are some missing persons. Although it is the story of an engaged couple and their impending marriage, the parents are *never* mentioned. This is astounding. Marriages were always arranged by the families and were really more of a social accomplishment for the parents than for the young people. But the names of the fathers of these two are found only in the genealogical tables. The mothers are never named.

We notice, also, that this young woman Mary seems to be terribly alone and on her own. If this is the case (and we will examine the evidence), it immediately accounts for her status as a bond slave. Youngsters that were orphans with no close relatives were simply given to any family that would house and feed them in return for their labor.

This was probably Mary's situation when the story opens. Such a status gives poignancy to her Son's remark later that He "came not to be served but to serve." Her lowly social status in no way reflects on her personal character or ancestry, for this girl was of royal blood, a descendant of David the king. But her status does remind us how powerless and poor among the nations Israel had become. It had been five hundred years since Israel had a king and a thousand years since the dynasty was founded by David.

Gabriel's Second Visit

Six months after Gabriel (the person in luminous clothing) was sent to Zacharias in the temple in Jerusalem, he was dispatched again, this time to Nazareth to a virgin engaged to a man whose name was Joseph, also a descendant of King David. The virgin's name was Mary (see Luke 1:26–28).

The multitude of paintings of the annunciation usually

show a beautiful girl sitting in a garden of lilies, apparently thinking elevated, poetic thoughts while white doves swirl around the garden. But it couldn't have been anything like that. In the first place, the words "came in unto her" would indicate that Gabriel found her in a house. And she undoubtedly was hard at work. Whatever their social status, the village women worked from dawn to dusk; if Mary were indeed an indentured servant, her work would be unending. Not only that, but since she had recently become engaged, she would be expected to begin to weave and sew the household goods that she would need for herself. This would have to be done in her "spare time." So Gabriel found her busy and alone. Visitors did not knock in those days unless it was late at night after the doors were barred. They simply stepped inside and called the name of the person they wished to see.

Now consider his greeting:

Hail, highly favored. The Lord is with thee. Blessed art thou among women.

Now *we* know what he was talking about, but is there anything in that sentence that could have given Mary any clue about the purpose of his visit? If you are a woman reading this, think back to when you were in high school (for that was Mary's approximate age) and imagine what you might have done or said if a strange visitor greeted you that way. Mary didn't say a silly word, or scream, or faint, or run away. She quietly "cast about in her mind," that is, she mentally touched all the bases to identify what this could refer to. She was not easily panicked, and she never spoke without thinking about it. This was remarkable self-possession in a teen-age girl. It was her habit to think things over carefully. Whether this was the result of a lifetime as a servant and the necessary self-discipline, we can't say. But Gabriel sees that for all her quiet and steady gaze she is frightened.

Fear not, Mary, for thou hast found favor with God. And, behold, [this word always introduces an astonishing thing] thou shalt conceive in thy womb, and bring forth a son, and shalt call his name JESUS.

It is almost certain that Gabriel was speaking to Mary in Aramaic, the Syro-Chaldaic dialect of Hebrew that had developed during Israel's captivity in Assyria and Babylonia. In the larger cities of Judea, many of the educated classes could read and speak Greek, even as today many of them know English as a second language. But among the Jews of the villages, the ordinary, everyday language was Aramaic. Most scholars agree that the Lord preached and talked in Aramaic. There are three places in the Gospel of Mark where you can read the exact Aramaic word He used (see Mark 5:41, 7:34, 14:36) As one commentator remarked, "When the Word was made flesh, He did not come speaking classical Greek, or even old Hebrew, but Aramaic." And there would have been neither opportunity nor occasion for a young girl in a small, mountain-hidden village to have learned Greek.

There was something, some implication in the Aramaic of Gabriel's last sentence that is not apparent in Luke's beautiful Greek narrative, for Mary is really startled. She understood him to mean (and she was not mistaken) that the conception would be "forthwith" or "immediately." If Gabriel had simply said, "You shall conceive and bear a son," as translated, she would have been pleased and thankful, for she certainly hoped that when she and Joseph were married that she would bear many sons. But the angel's message was something else—something immediate.

Now read Luke 1:26–38 again and notice that Gabriel talks for nine verses and Mary says just two sentences, which are as brief as they can possibly be. She didn't use an extra word, but she asked the obvious and practical question:

How can this be, seeing I know not a man?

Her question did not indicate doubt, but simply a desire for factual information. It is interesting to note that when Gabriel told Zacharias, Zacharias said, "It is too late," and Mary said, "It is too soon."

Because she believed (unlike Zacharias), Gabriel immediately gave her a beautiful and mysterious answer, "The power of the Highest shall overshadow thee." And then, to reward and strengthen her faith, he told her that Elisabeth, her aged cousin, was six months pregnant—to demonstrate that nothing is too hard for the Lord.

I think that after this last statement Gabriel simply stood and looked at Mary, and Mary stood and looked at Gabriel, until she realized that he was waiting for her consent. God never encroaches upon the human will or person. Her answer is typically brief:

Behold the handmaiden of the Lord. Be it unto me according to thy word [or you see before you a woman slave who belongs to the Lord. Let it be to me as you have said].

You know my name, Gabriel.
You know that I am a servant—
but I am the Lord's servant.

In a despised village
I am the least—
but David was my ancestor.

I am a have-not—
handmaid to hunger—
but I am The Woman.

Not Mother Eve, but I,
I am the Woman.
I stand at the crossroads
of the fullness of time.

Galatians 4:4

A Sudden Departure

The next day Mary must have wondered if she had dreamed the whole thing. After all, wasn't it a little preposterous that *she* would be chosen for this great honor? But in a week or two or three she had the proof within herself that indeed it was true. Her monthly cycle had stopped; she was pregnant.

And Mary arose in those days, and went into the hill country with haste, into the city of Juda; and entered the house of Zacharias, and saluted Elisabeth. Luke 1:39, 40.

In the sentence "and Mary arose" (Luke 1:39), we find an instance of a special usage. In that phrase, Luke means more than that she got out of bed, or that she stood up from a chair. Those would be the literal meanings, but the expression is more often used figuratively, to mean to come to a decision, to act in preparation, to make a radical change. This is the way the Lord used it in the story of the prodigal son. "When he came to himself, he said . . . *I will arise and go to my father*" (Luke 15:17, 18). He had finally come to a decision, and action was required. Here, Mary makes a decision that will necessitate action and a great change in her life.

Mary decided, probably for her own sake and for Elizabeth's, that she should go to her. There was a procedure for taking such a trip. She would have gone down to the well at daybreak some morning when she knew a caravan going to Jerusalem was being assembled. No one, not even a soldier, would travel alone, for it was too dangerous. Sometimes there would be several caravans forming at the well, watering animals, filling the water skins for the trip. All Mary had to do was simply arrive and walk with them anywhere in the train.

Here again she was terribly alone. It is almost inconceivable that if she had parents living, she would have been allowed to make such a trip. Parents were more careful and strict with their young daughters than parents are in our culture, and this was particularly true of an engaged girl. It was an unheard of thing that she was doing. It also sounds as though she had no closer female relative than Elizabeth. "His [Jesus'] mother's sister" is mentioned by John (19:25), but whether the "sister" was simply a kinswoman (cousin), older or younger, we have no information.

If Mary were traveling with a local caravan of Jewish people, they probably would have gone east across the high country about twenty-three miles to Galilee, crossed the Jordan at the Bridge of the Daughters of Jacob and gone south on the old Kings Highway through Perea, back across the Jordan at Jericho, and twenty miles up the steep switch-back road to Jerusalem. The trip would have been about eighty-five miles, much of it on dirt roads.

All of this round-about route was, of course, to avoid passing through the territory of the Samaritans. If the caravans were going due south through Samaria, it would have been only about sixty miles. Such travelers did not ride but used the donkeys as pack animals. Only Roman army officers of high rank rode horses, and a very high-born lady might travel in a litter or sedan chair. Everyone else expected to walk. That is what legs were for. When the emperor Hadrian visited Palestine he walked.

At Jerusalem the caravan would break up, with each traveler going his own way to relatives or business.

All we are told about the location of Zacharias's and Elisabeth's home is that it was in the "hill country of Judea." That would be somewhere in the country around Jerusalem. Some scholars have surmised that it might have been Hebron, for in Joshua 9:10, 11 it is mentioned that Hebron was given to the sons of Aaron to be a town for the priests. Others claim that tradition says that Zacharias's home was in Ein Karem, which was much closer to

Jerusalem, and also one of the "priests' villages." Ein
Karem is about five miles southwest on the Gaza road;
Hebron is about twenty-three miles due south on the road to
Beersheba. The whole journey took possibly four or five
days, depending on the route taken.

As was the custom, when Mary arrived at the house, she
simply stepped inside and called out Elisabeth's name. At
the sound of her voice, the Holy Spirit came upon Elisabeth
in a great infilling and also revealed to her what had happened to Mary. Elisabeth, inspired by the Holy Spirit,
blessed Mary and in the blessing mentioned the fact that
Mary had believed what Gabriel had told her. It is interesting
to note (we will need this later) that as far as the record goes
Mary never told a single person her great secret. God chose
and prepared a close-mouthed young woman who could
keep the greatest of all secrets.

In Luke 2:46–55 we have the only speech Mary ever
made. Elsewhere in the New Testament she speaks only in
single sentences. This passage is called "the Magnificat,"
from its first Latin word which means "I magnify," and it
is translated "My soul doth magnify the Lord." This beautiful and exalting song echoes Hannah's similar song in
I Samuel 2:1–10. Mary's Magnificat is inspired and pro-
phetic and is a shout of triumph. At this point it was pure,
unmixed joy.

> And Mary abode with her about three months, and returned
> to her own house. Luke 1:56.

Now anyone can add that up and see what happened.
Elisabeth had been six months along when Gabriel came to
Mary. It was not immediately but some time later that Mary
arose "in haste" to go to Elisabeth. So Elisabeth was close
to seven months along when Mary came. It is obvious that
Mary stayed three more months to wait for the birth of the
baby John. This would have been of help to Elisabeth—and

Mary must have been a wonderful help. But it was more than that. God was seeing to it that Mary had the graduate course in childbirth that she was going to need.

Down at the Well

So, when young John was about two or three weeks old, Mary came home again to Nazareth. She had left "in haste." No one knew why she had gone nor where. What an extraordinary thing for an engaged girl to do! She should have been weaving her linens. How perplexed Joseph and his family must have been. They had waited a week, and two weeks, and a month, and three months. Then, just as suddenly, she came back. But the worst for Joseph was still to come. In another month the whole town knew that Mary was with child.

Let's go down to the well, (now, ironically enough, called "Mary's Well"). The well was more than a place for water. It was the laundromat, the newspaper, the local club and the Mutual Aid Society. Here at the well, those who had happened to be on hand had seen Mary arrive with a little group of travelers. So they told the news that they were the first to know; Mary was back. Just a few weeks later the talk at the well was more somber—and secretive—and stopped when Mary arrived with her heavy water jar. We can guess what they said, since people have not changed much. Things like:

"Mary, of all people!"

"Do you suppose she has been abandoned by her lover?"

"Those quiet ones will fool you every time."

"Joseph looks just terrible—he is so thin and sad."

"Joseph's mother doesn't know a thing. I asked her right out."

The Stand-In

Joseph was having a very bad time. And well he might. Had she run to someone? Where was the father of the child now? In Matthew 1:18–25 you can read the story of Joseph's anguish. But God had chosen and prepared Joseph with as much care as He had chosen Mary. After all, this man was to be the stand-in for the Heavenly Father.

The custom was in those days that the announcement of the engagement was made in the synagogue with quite a ceremony, and afterward, the names were posted until the couple was actually married. This synagogue ceremony was so binding that it required a divorce to break it. There was no way a young couple could simply call it off; it was a contract between families.

After this announcement and the legal agreements concerning dowry and the like, there was a period of six months to a year in which the young couple accumulated the goods they would need to set up housekeeping. For those with wealthy parents who could help them, the time might be

quite brief. For working young people it could take months.
Joseph the carpenter very probably had started making the
wooden chests, tables, and benches they would need, as
Mary had started on the cloth weaving.

The terrible thing that happened to Joseph dragged his
pride in the dust. How humiliating—his espoused wife
away to another man. And, if Joseph had chosen her in
love, how heartbreaking that she would do this without
warning. The lovingly cut, pegged, and sanded wood of the
table he was making for them mocked him. A lesser man
would have thought only of vengeance. But it is a measure
of the man God chose that Joseph did not. Rather, he spent
sleepless nights wondering how he could break off the wedding plans without hurting the woman who betrayed him.

If Joseph had gone to the rabbi and asked for a divorce
because Mary was pregnant (and not by him), the rabbi was
bound by the law of Israel to have her stoned to death (Deut.
22:23, 24). There is a place back of Nazareth where this was
done at the foot of a little cliff. Joseph could not bring
himself to go to the rabbi. But if he did not get a divorce,
how could he live with her? Where and who was the other
man? Meanwhile, Mary had gone about her work—and
never told a soul. *Who would have believed her?*

Gabriel's Third Visit

One night, when Joseph finally fell asleep, worn out by
his dilemma, Gabriel appeared to him in a dream with a
message.

> Joseph, thou son of David, fear not to take unto thee
> Mary thy wife: for that which is conceived in her is of the
> Holy Ghost.
> And she shall bring forth a son, and thou shalt call his
> name JESUS: for he shall save his people from their sins.
> Matthew 1:20, 21.

From the text is it impossible to say dogmatically, but the next two verses may also be part of Gabriel's message rather than Matthew's explanation. If so, then Gabriel convinced Joseph by reminding him of Isaiah's prophecy about the virgin who would bear a child.

The next verse sounds as if Joseph got up immediately, went to the house where Mary was, and simply brought her home with him. Again, if Mary had had parents, this would have been impossible. At any rate, there *never was* a wedding feast in Nazareth for these two.

The custom was to have a fine social occasion when the two were ready to set up housekeeping. It was then that they stood under the *chuppah,* or wedding canopy. But this was not so much a religious ceremony as a joyful dinner party. The *chuppah* is a very old custom and is mentioned in Isaiah. At any rate, months later when they left for Bethlehem Mary was still called his "espoused" wife (Luke 2:5). I rather suspect that Nazareth was quite upset with these two.

Down at the well the next day the gossips were really perplexed and indignant.

"So! It *was* Joseph's baby after all. They must have had a very severe lover's quarrel to make her run away like that."

One more note: this painful situation was necessary. If God had chosen an unengaged girl, who would have married her? And if He had chosen a newly married girl, who would ever have believed her a virgin? But she said that she was, Gabriel said she was, and Joseph knew she was.

Micah Was Right

What a relief it must have been to Mary to have Joseph know the truth by a message from God by Gabriel. Gabriel had given them a check point to verify their strange experiences to each other. To both he had said, "His name will be JESUS," so they knew they had not been imagining things. Moreover, when Gabriel told Joseph to name the child, he appointed him surrogate father, for naming was the privilege of the father. Remember when Elisabeth tried to name her baby John? The friends would not accept it until Zacharias wrote it himself.

The next three or four months must have been both difficult and wonderful as Mary and Joseph suffered the disapproval of Nazareth, and shared the marvel that was happening to Mary. They surely knew that Micah had prophesied that the Messiah would be born in Bethlehem. They must have wondered why God had not chosen a couple in Bethlehem. (There seems to have been a good reason for this that we will discuss later.) They must have wondered if they should go to Bethlehem. But these two knew that this was God's business that they were involved in and they had character enough to wait and see what God would do, being convinced He could manage His own affairs.

By Decree of Augustus

One day a squad of Roman soldiers, led by an officer on horseback, came through the village. Down at the well they stopped long enough to post the emperor's decree. Augustus, emperor of the known world, had decided to take a census of his empire. Every man would return to his ancestral home for the counting and head tax. Joseph and Mary had not imagined that God would move the entire population of the far-flung empire to get them to Bethlehem. It must have been an amazing sort of fruit-basket-upset time, for everywhere people began packing up and making plans (and some had to make *long* journeys) in order to comply.

Historians say it took a full two years and possibly longer to move everyone and get the machinery of enrollment in motion. For Mary and Joseph it would be simplicity itself. They were both descended from David—they would both be enrolled in Bethlehem. They packed everything. They had no intention of returning, as we shall later see.

This time they could have moved with a large caravan of local people going to various towns in Judea and Perea. This was the third time Mary made the five-day walk during her nine months. Down to Ein Karem and back, 130 miles; down to Bethlehem via Jerusalem, another 85 miles; total 215 miles since she first knew she was with child. She was not only a quiet girl, she was a strong and healthy girl, undaunted by unusual circumstances. As the caravan moved south of Jerusalem, Joseph and Mary would notice that they were in sheep country, the very hills and valley where their ancestor David had watched his father's sheep and written his songs. Bethlehem is only five and a half miles south of Jerusalem, an easy walk, even leading a donkey loaded with all your camping gear.

O Little Town . . . !

When the small town of Bethlehem came into view, sprawling up the southwest slope of the hill, it was a bee-hive of activity. So many descendants of the original settlers had arrived that the place was quite beside itself trying to absorb them all. Here we must note a couple of facts that will help us understand the subsequent events. In the first place, if Mary and Joseph had had a single relative in Bethlehem, the relatives would have been duty-bound to take them in. We must conclude that they had *no* relatives in the town. Later we will see a probable explanation. In the second place, the inn, long so infamous for being over-crowded at the wrong moment in history, has a most interesting history.

The Infamous Inn

In the story of David we find that when he became king of Israel, he decided to give his own place in Bethlehem to Chimham, the son of a loyal friend called Barzillai (II Sam. 19:37-39). Whether this was the old farmhouse where David was born, we are not told. Or why David, the youngest of eight sons, would have inherited it, we do not know. It is possible, of course, that he had asserted his rights as king and appropriated the house. At any rate, David *did* give a house in Bethlehem to Chimham. But Chimham did not need another house and did not want to live in Bethlehem, so he made the house into an inn for travelers on their way to Egypt (Jer. 41:17).

Now a town the size of Bethlehem would not have had

more than one travelers' inn. Even if the original buildings were gone, (although there are stone houses of remarkable antiquity around there to this day) it is barely possible that Mary and Joseph applied for refuge at the old farmhouse, or on the site of the old farmhouse where David had been born. Ironically, they found it too full to accept the pregnant mother of David's greater Son. If so, this gives new meaning to the words found in the prologue of John's gospel where he says:

> He came to His own things [literal] and His own things received Him not. John 1:11.

The Sheepfold

But where they did find refuge was much better for their purposes and for God's. Because the shepherds were still out in the fields overnight, the large communal sheepfold on the edge of the town was unoccupied. This explains a lot of puzzling things, as we shall see. Mary and Joseph must have made camp in the cave of the shepherds. They were used to camping; they had camped all the way down from Nazareth and to live in a limestone cave was not considered a hardship. Some of these caves are almost snow white inside, carpeted in fine white sand. The shepherds knew that a young couple who were expecting a child any day were camped in their fold. How do I know this?

When Gabriel told the shepherds that they would find the babe "wrapped in swaddling clothes lying in a manger," the shepherds knew at once *where* and *which* manger held the child. In Bethlehem to this day there are dozens of mangers. Every household has a few sheep and a donkey. Nearly every family has a stone-carved or wooden (more rarely) manger on the side or back of the house for pet animals. If the shepherds had not known immediately of the situation in their fold, they would have had to look in many, many mangers. But they must have known and given permission to the young couple to shelter there, because if the weather turned cold, they would have had to evict them or let the couple share their shelter with the flocks of sheep. But God was making those arrangements and He is in charge of the weather.

Nowhere does the text say or even imply that Mary and Joseph arrived in Bethlehem the evening before the birth. God was tenderly, moment by moment watching over that young mother-to-be. Luke says quite specifically, "While they were there." They may have been there two or three weeks before the birth took place.

> And so it was [this is how it happened], that, while they were there [and Joseph was going daily to stand in line for the enrolling], the days were accomplished that she should be delivered. [Paul says in Gal. 4:4 that God sent His Son "when the fulness of time was come," meaning at an exact, predetermined date on God's calendar.] And she brought forth her firstborn son, and [she] wrapped him in swaddling clothes, and [she] laid him in a manger; for there was no room for them in the inn. Luke 2:6-7.

The Greek of this passage implies that she gave birth without help and herself wrapped Him and prepared His bed in the manger. It astonishes most people to find that there is no mention of a barn or oxen or doves. All of those details came from the storytellers of medieval times in Europe who could not imagine a manger except in connection with a wooden cattle barn.

The Angel of the Lord

> And there were in the same country shepherds abiding in the field [or camping out in the grazing grounds], keeping watch over their flock by night. And, lo [this always means

great surprise], the angel of the Lord came upon them [this is another arrival of Gabriel, the man in the luminous clothing], and the glory of the Lord shone around about them: and they were sore afraid. [They were almost scared to death. Every time Gabriel arrives with a message, he first must reassure and calm the terrified recipients.] And the angel said unto them, Fear not: for, behold, [the same word as "lo" and means consider a most amazing thing], I bring you good tidings of great joy, which shall be to all people. For unto you is born this day ["unto us a child is born, unto us a son is given," Isa. 9:6] in the city of David a Saviour, which is Christ the Lord ["the Messiah-Jehovah" in Hebrew]. And this shall be a sign unto you; ye shall find the babe wrapped in swaddling clothes, lying in a manger. [Gabriel had just told them that the young couple's expected baby has been born and laid in their feeding trough, wrapped as all babies were.] And suddenly there was with the angel a multitude of the heavenly host praising God, and saying, Glory to God in the highest, and on earth peace, good will toward men. Luke 2:8-14.

The Heavenly Host

Please, notice that there is nothing here about the angels singing. Perhaps they did, but Luke records that they were praising God and *saying*. Here, again, the angel of the Lord is not named, but I cannot imagine that on this tremendous occasion anyone less than Gabriel (who has been involved from the beginning) would be sent. Because of Christmas card art we visualize the angel flying overhead, but on the other occasions, to Daniel, to Zacharias, to Mary, to Cornelius, he stood beside them to deliver the message. I think it must have been so here. Phillips translates this passage, "The angel of the Lord stood by their side."

The multitudes of angels were thronging the Judean hillsides, talking and shouting of the glory of God. How amazing that He would so express His attitude of generous and gracious giving toward the human race, His good will toward all people. This birth proved that some day God would bring, by this child, perfect peace to the troubled earth.

The angels also had another reason for being there. They had been commanded to go and worship.

> When he bringeth in the firstbegotten into the world, he saith, And let all the angels of God worship him. Hebrews 1:6.

And:

> ... God was manifest in the flesh, justified in the Spirit, seen of angels. ... I Timothy 3:16.

The angels must have been astounded that they were allowed to worship God without the Light Unapproachable, and wrapped in swaddling clothes.

> And [when] ... the angels were gone away from them into heaven, the shepherds said one to another, Let us now go even unto Bethlehem, and see this thing which is come to pass, which the Lord hath made known unto us. And they came with haste [the shepherds' fields were probably those that lie east and slightly north of Bethlehem], and [they] found Mary, and Joseph, and the babe (lit., new-born child] lying in a manger. Luke 2:15, 16.

Why Shepherds?

Sometimes it has been asked why this wonder was told to a bunch of lowly shepherds. Why wasn't the mayor of Bethlehem notified?

There are at least three reasons. First, the shepherds were the hosts to the family and knew of the situation. Second, they were awake and in a place with space enough to accommodate the "multitude of the heavenly host." Also, it was eminently suitable that the Lamb of God should be born in a sheepfold. And the shepherds had the privilege of telling Mary and Joseph about the visitation of the angels. There is no hint that Mary and Joseph knew anything about this. They might have noticed the light in the sky, but, after all, they had reason to be preoccupied. When the shepherds arrived, all out of breath from running, they were not surprised to find that the baby had been born just as Gabriel had said.

Someday, an artist who has wandered around the hills of Bethlehem will paint a picture of the scene like this: The perspective will be from deep in a cave, looking toward a wide opening. In the foreground will be Joseph sitting before a campfire warming some food for Mary. Along the righthand side of the cave will be a long feeding trough carved into the soft, white limestone. In this manger trough will be fresh straw, and on a blanket on the straw, a bundle looking very, very small in its close, white wrappings. Beside Him, on the floor on a pile of blankets, a tired young woman will be sitting, leaning her head against the manger. Beyond all three, framed in the deep royal blue of the predawn sky, will shine the morning star, a glowing ball of white fire (Luke 1:78; II Peter 1:19; Rev. 2:28, 28:16).

Getting Out the News

After Mary, Joseph, and the shepherds exchanged what information they had about this wonderful baby, it is recorded:

> When they had seen it, they made known abroad the saying which was told them concerning this child. And all they that heard it wondered at those things which were told them by the shepherds. Luke 2:17, 18.

The shepherds knocked on every door in Bethlehem with the great news. A promise of God to Bethlehem that was five hundred years old (Mic. 5:2) had been kept. Consider also who were in Bethlehem: men and families from all over the Roman Empire. God had arranged the enrolling so that when these people went home, they could tell and retell to their own Jewish communities what God had done—and most of all, that they had seen the baby with their own eyes. The scandal of Nazareth was the pride of Bethlehem.

Was there a person in Bethlehem who did not want to see that baby? I feel a little sorry for Mary. The next day must have been a long, tiring day as the stream of visitors kept coming. What did the quiet girl do?

> But Mary kept all these things, and pondered them in her heart. Luke 2:19 (see also v. 51).

Mary's heart became a treasure chest in which she cherished all the wonderful things that Gabriel had said to her and to Joseph and now to the shepherds. And she turned them over in her mind as another woman might have counted her jewels. It was all joy.

The Treasure Chest

One week and a day later, the whole town turned out for the great occasion of the circumcising ceremony that made Him a Son of the Covenant which God made with Abraham and which also obligated Him to keep the whole law. But this time it was different. Thousands, probably by this time millions, of Jewish boys had been circumcised as a sign of their special relationship to the God of Israel—but not one had ever kept the law of God. This One would, and no one after Him in this age would ever do it again.

... made of a woman, made under the law, to redeem them that were under the law.... Galatians 4:4, 5.

"Now Let Me Die"

Thirty-two days later, when the baby was forty days old, Mary, Joseph, and Jesus made the short five-and-a-half-mile trip back to the Temple in Jerusalem. The law required that on the fortieth day after childbirth an offering be made for a firstborn male and an offering of cleansing for the mother (Lev. 12:2–8).

As the young couple came into the outer court, looking about for a priest to officiate for them at the altar (for this was their first experience with this offering, and they were villagers), they were met by an old man named Simeon. Old Simeon was a student of the Scriptures who knew from the Book of Daniel that it was time for the Messiah. Since he had no access to the records of old Babylon, whose calendar only roughly corresponded to the Hebrew calendar, Simeon had no way of knowing *exactly* when the decree went forth (Dan. 9:25) to rebuild Jerusalem in the days of Nehemiah. But he knew that it had been approximately 450 years, so the time was up.

So persistent had been Simeon's pursuit of the Scriptures that God promised him that He would let him live to see the Messiah. But Simeon's problem was complicated by some seemingly contradictory prophecies. Micah had said the Messiah-Ruler would come out of Bethlehem (Mic. 5:2). Malachi had said, ''And the Lord, whom ye seek, shall suddenly come to his temple'' (Mal. 3:1). Simeon may have expected the Messiah to arrive in Jerusalem as a conquering hero.

On this morning the Spirit of God had told Simeon that today was the day, and to go to the temple and wait; the Messiah would come. Was Simeon astonished to find that He was a baby in the arms of His mother?

> Then he took him up in his arms, and blessed God, and said, Lord, now lettest thou thy servant depart in peace, according to thy word: for mine eyes have seen thy salvation [salvation is not an abstract; salvation is a Person], which thou hast prepared before the face of all people; a light to lighten the Gentiles, and the glory of thy people Israel. Luke 2:28–32.

Joseph and Mary were amazed at what Simeon said. Mary

remembered every word. Then Simeon added a sharp, heavy, black stone to the jewels in the treasure chest of Mary's heart.

(*Yea,* a sword shall pierce through thine own soul also,) that the thoughts of many hearts may be revealed. Luke 2:35.

Her heart *also?* Who else would be pierced?

An Old Puzzle

Many Bible students through the centuries have been puzzled by the statement in Luke 2:39 that Joseph, Mary, and the baby returned to Nazareth right after they had finished the ceremonies of His birth, when Jesus was forty days old. Where does the flight into Egypt fit in?

Some have suggested that the wise men found Him in Nazareth. However, that "solution" is impossible for a number of reasons. First, Matthew plainly states that the wise men went to Bethlehem and found Him there. If they had been redirected to Nazareth and found Him there, then Gabriel's warning, and the midnight departure for Egypt, were totally unnecessary. No soldiers came to Nazareth; no babies died in Nazareth. Had Jesus been there he would have been perfectly safe. If the wise men had been in Nazareth it would not have been necessary for them to go home by "another route" to avoid Herod. The main highway from Bethlehem does go through Jerusalem, but the highway from Nazareth goes east to Galilee—sixty miles north of Jerusalem.

The obvious solution is that Joseph and Mary with the baby made a trip to Nazareth immediately after the ceremonies of His birth were taken care of. They returned to gather up any possessions they had left behind when they went for the enrolling. Now they planned a permanent move. The wonderful events of His birth had convinced them that David's greater Son should be reared in David's town. There is human motivation, too. In Nazareth Mary and Joseph were a scandal—living together without a wedding feast. In Bethlehem they were the parents of the Great King. Luke simply omits everything that happened between the first return shortly after His birth and the second return to Nazareth after the stay in Egypt. In chapter 11 you will find more details about this.

PART TWO
Historical Flashback

David and Bathsheba
and the Sword

Historical events do not happen in a vacuum. Human events always have roots in what has gone on before. To understand Simeon's ominous words about the sword and its connection with the newborn King, we must retell the old story of David and Bathsheba and of the curse on Coniah. And to clearly understand prophecy concerning Israel, we should have a fix on the time of the King's birth.

* * *

It did not seem such a big thing to King David. It was the turn of the year; the crops were in; it was the "time when kings go forth to battle"; but David had not gone with his army. The soldiers were over in Amman (now the capital of Jordan) under General Joab. David, the mightiest warrior of them all, for some unexplained reason, had stayed home. This evening he paced on the roof of the palace. Below him, in the garden of a little house that backed right up to the wall of the palace, was a small pool, a fountain, and a beautiful young woman taking a bath. He watched unobserved. Then he inquired who lived behind the palace. He learned that it was the home of Uriah the Hittite who had married a Jewish girl named Bathsheba, and had become one of David's best warriors. David sent a messenger to bring the girl to the palace.

There had already been many women in David's life. His first wife was Michal, the daughter of King Saul; then Abigail the beautiful; and eight more legal wives, beside concubines and women sent as pledges of political friendship from the neighboring kings. He had a house full of beautiful women. One more woman and one more night did not seem to him so big a thing.

He probably felt like the man whom Henry VIII tortured and killed for having been a youthful lover of Katherine Howard. He said, "The maid was willing, and it was a summer night—so small a thing to die for!"

David had no intention of stealing Uriah's wife. He really wanted only a sample of her charms, so it came as an irritating complication when she sent word that, because of their one night, she was with child. David thought of a very clever solution to the problem: send for Uriah for news of the battle. Let him have a week's leave. He would stay with his beautiful young wife and would never suspect that their child had royal blood.

Sergeant Uriah

Unfortunately for David he had badly underestimated Uriah. Uriah reported, all right, and gave the king a detailed account of the campaign. Then, David said, "Now you deserve a good rest. Go home, and I'm sending over a fine dinner for you and your wife."

But Uriah slept at the door of the king's house with all the servants of his lord, and went not down to his house. And when they had told David, saying, Uriah went not down unto his house, David said unto Uriah, Camest thou not from thy journey? why then didst thou not go down unto thine house? And Uriah said unto David, The ark, and Israel, and Judah, abide in tents; and my lord Joab, and the servants of my lord, are encamped in the open fields; shall I then go into mine house, to eat and to drink, and to lie with my wife? as thou livest, and as thy soul liveth, I will not do this thing. II Samuel 11:9-11.

David had run head on into the zeal of a proselyte; proselytes were often much more loyal than the native-born. Also, the man who does not curb his appetites is always baffled by the man who can and does. So David invited him to eat at the royal table that evening and saw to it that Uriah had much too much to drink. When Uriah was very drunk, the king urged him again to go home to his wife, and again he refused and stayed in the servants' quarters overnight.

The next morning when Uriah came as commanded to get a message for General Joab, David had a sealed letter ready. Uriah carried in his tunic his own death warrant, for David's letter instructed Joab to see to it that Uriah was killed in battle. And so he was. Joab did not yet know why David wanted Uriah out of the way, but he must have realized the truth immediately when he came home and found Bathsheba as one of the King's wives. Perhaps some of the people felt that David had done a very noble thing to marry the young widow and care for her.

So David's sin was buried, he thought, in a foreign grave with Uriah. He had not only forgotten "Thou shalt not covet thy neighbor's wife" (Exod. 20:17), he had also ignored the fact that "all things are naked and opened unto the eyes of him with whom we have to do" (Heb. 4:13). The Scriptures now add: "But the thing that David had done displeased the Lord" (II Sam. 11:27). Bathsheba had her child, and it must have been an exceptionally promising baby boy, for David loved the child deeply.

A Higher Court

Then, David had a visit from Nathan the prophet. Nathan told a story about a grave injustice that had been done in David's realm. A very rich man with thousands of sheep and cattle had stolen his poor neighbor's one pet lamb to make a dinner for his guests.

David was outraged! The story particularly touched David because as a shepherd boy he had had several pet lambs and loved them very much. His judgment on the offender was severe and in two parts: (1) the rich man was to pay back four lambs for the one he had stolen; and (2) the rich man was to be executed because of his sheer cruelty.

Then Nathan said, "*You* are the man."

In a blinding flash of insight that cut like a sword, David saw what he had done as God saw it. He had pronounced his own sentence. God knew that David could not be executed, because although he had "killed Uriah with the sword of the Ammonities," it would be hard to prove by the law. Also, there was not a man in Israel who could or would have carried out the execution of David. Furthermore, God knew that David's execution would punish Israel more than David. So the sentence was:

Now therefore the sword shall never depart from thine house. II Samuel 12:10.

The other part of the sentence about restoring fourfold began to be executed immediately. Bathsheba's baby, whom David loved, died almost at once. Then, Absalom killed his brother Amnon, and Absalom was in turn killed, breaking David's heart.

> O my son Absalom, my son, my son, Absalom! would God
> I had died for thee, O Absalom, my son, my son! II Samuel
> 18:33.

And finally, Solomon killed the oldest brother Adonijah. So David lost four sons because of Uriah.

The Sword

Satan is a murderer (John 8:44) and he soon realized that God had taken away the hedge of protection from the house of David. He was, no doubt, only too happy to oblige. This, by the way, is one illustration of how God uses the malice of Satan to carry out what is known as "the negative side of the will of God."

With all those wives and concubines who had produced many sons to survive him, one would think that David's descendants would be numerous indeed. And so they were for a generation or two, but then, the pruning with the sword began in earnest.

Nearly two hundred years later, when the nation was divided into a northern kingdom, Israel, and a southern kingdom, Judea, a man named Jehu, a general, not of royal blood, became king of Israel. Today, his maneuver would be considered a typical army takeover, a coup, a putsch.

> And it came to pass, when the letter came to them, that they
> [Jehu and his soldiers] took the king's [Ahab's] sons, and
> slew SEVENTY PERSONS, and put their heads in baskets,
> and sent them to Jezreel. II Kings 10:7.
> So Jehu slew all that remained of the house of Ahab in
> Jezreel, and all his great men, and his kinsfolks, and his
> priests, until he left him none remaining. II Kings 10:11.

Then,

> Jehu met with the brethern of Ahaziah king of Judah, and
> said, Who are ye? And they answered, We are the brethren
> of Ahaziah [Princes of Judah]; and we go down to salute the
> children of the king and the children of the queen. And he
> [Jehu] said, Take them alive. And they took them alive, and
> slew them at the pit of the shearing house, even *two and
> forty men;* neither left he any of them. II Kings 10:13, 14.

Jezebel's Daughter

In the above quoted passages you have read how Jehu
managed to systematically wipe out practically all the descendants of David who were in Israel and in Judea. But
there were a few survivors.

Then came Athaliah, daughter of Jezebel and Ahab, who
combined all the worst features of her infamous parents.

> And when Athaliah the mother of Ahaziah saw that her son
> was dead, she arose and destroyed all the seed royal. II
> Kings 11:1.

She certainly meant to; she thought she had. But there was
one small boy, Joash, less than a year old, who was smug-
gled out of the nursery where all the royal children were
slaughtered like lambs. Little Joash was hid with his nurse
in the temple of the Lord for six years. The temple was one
place where Athaliah never went. So now the house of
David that had been so numerous was reduced to little Joash
and at least one other descendant. The genealogies indicate
that there was somewhere, maybe in the captivity in Assyria, at least one contemporary of Joash who was also
descended from David the king.

Nevertheless, God had given David an unconditional
promise that someday there would be a child who would be
one of his natural descendants but (most astonishing) He

would be the Son of God, and would be King forever (II Sam. 7:16, Ps. 2:7, Luke 1:31–33).

Along with this promise the relentless, pursuing sword continued to cut down David's house for nearly a thousand years. The last victim of the sentence on David was the promised King, David's greater son. There, at the cross, when a Roman soldier buried his spear in the Lord's side, the sword of judgment on David's house was finally satisfied and David's sin atoned for (John 19:33). The "Lamb that was slain before the foundation of the world" would turn out to be David's greater son. He died for David's sin, too, or there could have been no forgiveness, and no Psalm 51.

These are some of the facets of the Christmas story that bear pondering: that Mary seemed so alone; that God chose a young couple in Nazareth as though there were no descendants of David in Bethlehem; that Mary and Joseph did not have a single family of relatives in Bethlehem to stay with when they came. It all adds up to the possibility that there may have been very few descendants of David left, and fewer still who were of an age and character to take this enormous responsibility. It is entirely possible that Mary and Joseph were the sole survivors of the royal house of King David.

The Curse on Coniah and All the King's Men

As if David's sin and the pursuing sword were not enough, God Himself made the situation absolutely impossible when He pronounced a curse on Coniah, son of King Jehoiakim. Until we know this story, we have no idea of what an incredible miracle Christmas was.

The Most Wicked King

In the sixth century B.C. the king of Judah (the south half of Israel) was a man named Jehoiakim, and he was a man of extraordinary evil.

> He did that which was evil in the sight of the Lord.... II Kings 23:37.

Jehoiakim had many wicked forebears in the kingly line who had deliberately led Israel into every detestable practice of the Canaanites, but he added to their sensual sins a most unusual insult to the God of Israel. For this, a specific curse was pronounced upon his son Coniah.

Henry II, King of England, had his Thomas á Becket, and Henry VIII had his Sir Thomas More, and both kings managed to dispose of these men who plagued them like a bad conscience. Jehoiakim, King of Judah, had Jeremiah, who was not quite so easily disposed of. All during Jehoiakim's eleven-year reign in Jerusalem, the Babylonian army was harassing his land and threatening the destruction of his city. Jeremiah was no comfort ot the king.

Jeremiah was called the "weeping Prophet" because the Lord had revealed to him that which was going to happen: that the land and the city would be taken by Nebuchadnezzar, the city destroyed, and the people killed or made captives. So when Jeremiah preached, he wept. (No one should preach impending judgment without tears. If you hear someone pronouncing doom and enjoying doing it, you can be very sure God has not sent him. When the Lord Jesus pronounced another judgment on Jerusalem in the days of Rome, He wept over the city—Luke 19:41).

"Signet Ring"

Jehoiakim could not believe that any of Jeremiah's prophecies would be fulfilled. He continued his idolatrous practices, but also insisted that since the children of Israel were Jehovah's chosen people, they would be automatically protected from judgment no matter what they did.

Seven years before Jehoiakim became king, when he was about eighteen years old, his first son was born, and Jehoiakim named him Jeconiah. *Je* is a verbal shorthand for Jehovah, and *Coniah* means "to establish." Jehoiakim believed that since God has established the kingdom of Israel, both he and his son would be absolutely secure in their kingships. But God, in the two times he addressed Jeconiah directly, with fine irony called him only *Coniah,* and said,

> As I live, saith the Lord, though Coniah, the son of Jehoiakim king of Judah were the signet [ring] upon my right hand, yet would I pluck thee thence; and I will give thee [Coniah] into the hand of . . . [the] king of Babylon. Jeremiah 22:24, 25.

But that was not all; there were two more chilling prophecies, one for Jehoiakim and one for Coniah.

So to stop this demoralizing preaching, Jehoiakim put Jeremiah in prison. He was afraid to kill him just then. God still desired to postpone the judgment and show mercy on Israel, so He spoke to Jeremiah in prison and Jeremiah dictated the message to Baruch the scribe.

The Unpardonable Sin

When this message of warning was presented to the king by some of his nobles, this is what happened:

> And Jehudi read it in the ears of the king, and in the ears of all the princes which stood beside the king. Now the king sat in the winterhouse in the ninth month, and there was a fire on the hearth burning before him. And it came to pass, that when Jehudi had read three or four leaves, he [Jehoiakim] cut it [the scroll] with the penknife, and cast it into the fire that was on the hearth, until all the roll was consumed in the fire. . . . Nevertheless Elnathan and Delaiah and Gemariah had made intercession to the king that he would not burn the roll: but he would not hear them. Jeremiah 36:21–25.

Jehoiakim's Sentence

So what did God do about this? Jeremiah 36:27 says, "Then the word of the Lord came to Jeremiah, after that the king had burned the roll, . . . saying,"

Take thee another roll, and write in it all the former words that were in the first roll, which Jehoiakim . . . hath burned. And thou shalt say to Jehoiakim king of Judah, Thus said the Lord; Thou hast burned this roll . . . therefore thus saith the Lord of Jehoiakim king of Judah; He shall have none to sit upon the throne of David: and his [Jehoiakim's] dead body shall be cast out in the day to the heat, and in the night to the frost. Jeremiah 36:28–30.

They shall not lament for him, saying, Ah, my brother! . . . Ah, lord! or Ah, his glory! He shall be buried with the burial of an ass, drawn and cast forth beyond the gates of Jerusalem. Jeremiah 22:18, 19.

To be *not* buried was the ultimate indignity, a horrible thing to the Jews. To have one's carcass treated like a dead donkey and left for the buzzards and wild dogs was just unthinkable. But this is what happened to the man who tried to destroy the word of God. Then concerning Jehoiakim's son Coniah, God added a most dramatic note.

Coniah's Curse

O earth, earth, earth, hear the word of the Lord. Thus saith the Lord, Write ye this man childless, a man that shall not prosper in his days: for no man of his seed shall prosper, sitting upon the throne of David, and ruling any more in Judah. Jeremiah 22:29, 30.

Incredible! God had chosen among the sons of David and had said that the right to the throne would be vested in Solomon and his line, and Coniah was the inheritor of that line. Now, no descendant of his could ever prosper on the throne. "Write ye this man childless" meant that in God's sight he might as well be childless, for God would not accept any offspring of his (he already had children). Joseph of Nazareth was the direct descendant of Coniah (Matt. 1:6,

11, 16); *he was under the curse should he ever try to be king.* His sons: James, Judah, Joseph (Jr.), and Simon (Matt. 13:55) were also inheritors of that curse.

But Mary was descended from David through his son Nathan. Nathan's line had no right to the throne, but it had the blood of David as truly as did Solomon's line. In Mary the Lord Jesus inherited the blood line of David; in Joseph, by legal adoption, He inherited the legal right to the throne without the curse, because He is not of the "seed" of Joseph or Coniah. This is the only means whereby there could ever again be a king in Israel. God put a lock on the throne that only He could open. There is only one Jew alive who can claim David's throne; He sits at God's right hand.

One more note: when the temple was burned by the armies of Titus in 70 A.D., all the records of the tribes and families that were kept in the temple were destroyed. In the providence of God, Matthew and Luke had already reproduced Joseph's and Mary's genealogies. That means that no other Israelite can ever claim the throne of David by inheritance: no one but Jesus of Nazareth, whose mother's and foster-father's royal rights are now published in over twelve hundred languages.

What Year? What Month?
What Time of Day?

When we were schoolchildren, history could have been a most dramatic and exciting story—except for the dates to be memorized. I never remember anyone when I was a child and a student, or when I was a history teacher myself, who really *liked* learning dates. But sometimes it is extremely important to know when something occurred; it may make all the difference. And I have the profound conviction that most of the great turning points of history could have happened at no other time. There always seemed to be a converging of forces, of peoples, of ideas, even of climate changes that made the great important things happen when they did.

In the case of our story of the birth of Christ it turns out that it is of utmost importance to know exactly when it happened. Both of the chroniclers of the event, Matthew and Luke, dated their documents according to the practice of the times, by the reigning kings and governors. More importantly, Paul, writing by inspiration, says, "That in the fullness of time, God sent forth His Son, made of a woman . . . '' The idiom "fullness of time" means at the exact predestined moment. In God's foreordained scheme of things the birth took place precisely on schedule.

The Record Made

At the time of the birth there was a record made in Bethlehem, because that was the custom. There was also a record made in Jerusalem when the baby was forty days old. On that day the child had to be presented in the temple. The offerings were made for the cleansing of the mother, and for the child, because He was a first-born male (Luke 2:23, 24; Lev. 12:2-8). At that time the genealogies of both Mary and Joseph were found in the library of the temple, and the new name was added to the scroll. Matthew records *Joseph's* line from David, and Luke records *Mary's* line from David.

In Matthew, because the author is writing the story of the Great King, the line is traced back to King David and to Abraham. There is a specific difference made in the record of this birth. Of all Joseph's progenitors it says "begat," but of the Lord Jesus it is very exact in noting that Joseph was not the begettor, but was simply "the husband of Mary of whom was born Jesus" (Matt. 1:16).

Luke's beautiful account of the birth makes the same distinction. Because Luke writes the story of the Perfect Man, the genealogy is traced all the way back to Adam, the first man. But when Luke comes to this birth, he says, "Jesus . . . who was 'legally reckoned' the son of Joseph" (Luke 3:23). That is what the words "as was supposed" mean in this context.

The Records Destroyed

Just seventy years after the birth of Christ, Jerusalem was destroyed by the armies of Rome under Titus Vespasianus, and the temple was burned with all its records. The only genealogies saved were these that have been preserved in the Gospels.

Jerusalem became a non-Jewish city following this holocaust and was destroyed again in 132–135 A.D. to end another rebellion. To Rome, both Jew and Christian were problems to be severely dealt with. No one was concerned about determining the date of birth of the Jewish Messiah who had been rejected by His own people and executed by the Romans.

Dionysius Exiguus

It was in 543 A.D. by our calendar that the most famous of all the emperors of the Eastern Roman Empire, Flavius Anicus Justianus, surnamed "The Great," commissioned the Scythian monk Dionysius Exiguus to fix the date of the Great Event on the Roman calendar. Five and one-half centuries is more than half a millennium, and a long time on any calendar.

To make the calculation, Exiguus had to work with some of the worst calendars of western civilization. The old Roman calendars were far from being synchronized with the solar year and had to be continually altered and adjusted. Whole months, called intercalary months, were added at times. Occasionally days and weeks were omitted. The names of the months were changed, and moreover, the emperors liked to have everything dated from their own ascendancy to the throne.

Exiguus labored long and well, apparently alone. After innumerable and painstaking calculations he concluded that Christ's birth, the date from which all future dates would be computed in the now-Christianized West, occurred 753 years after the founding of Rome by Romulus. To the Jews this was 3,760 years after the creation of Adam. To the Greeks this corresponded to the year of the 194th Olympiad.

We think of it as the year zero, but there is no such year. One B.C. stands contiguous to 1 A.D., with no room to turn around in.

This accounts for one year of Exiguus's error. Christ could not have been born in year one *before* Christ or year one *after* Christ; there must be a year between as the year of the birth. Apparently Exiguus overlooked this small point. He also omitted a period of about four and a half years during which one of the emperors ruled as a regent during his father's lifetime.

In spite of the poor records with which he was forced to work, Exiguus came within six years of the actual year, and that is astonishingly close. The immediate result of this error was to obscure, for another fifteen centuries, the facts about the astronomical event that sent the Magi to Palestine. Nevertheless, we owe a great debt to Dionysius Exiguus, accomplished mathematician and astronomer, for if he had not given us an approximate date, it would have been a much harder task to determine an accurate date later.

Between Matthew and Luke

That the actual date is important is apparent from the records of public accountant Levi and Dr. Luke; both dated their accounts. Public accountant Levi was Matthew who gave up the tax service of Rome to become an spostle. He dated his account with reference to the reigning kings, as did all historians of the day.

> Now when Jesus was born in Bethlehem of Judea in the days of *Herod the king* . . . Matthew 2:1.

Josephus, in his description of Herod's death, tells us that it was on March 13, 4710 according to the Julian calendar;[1] we call it 4 B.C. So the birth of the Lord had to be before 4 B.C. while Herod was still alive. Dr. Luke, in his account, also gives us a date.

This taxing was first made when Cyrenius was governor of Syria. Luke 2:2.

For many years historians assumed that Luke was in error here. The only governorship of P. Sulpicius Quirinius in the records started in 7 A.D., which was much too late by any reckoning. But first in Antioch, and more recently, in Ankara, Turkey, were found the inscriptions that proved that Quirinius (Cyrenius is the Anglicized spelling) had indeed served as governor of Syria starting in 8 B.C. for several years as the legate of Emperor Augustus, in the days of Saturnius the proconsul.

This was in 8 B.C., so Christ's birth had to be after 8 B.C. and before 4 B.C. Approximately 6 B.C. would be the median of these two dates and a reasonably close estimate of the precise time.

Not only the year but the time of year was in error. December 25 was chosen, because that was the date on which the pagans celebrated "Dies Invictus Natalis" (Birthday of the Unconquered); on that date it became apparent that the sun, which had been retreating ever southward, had reversed its course. It was reborn; there would be another spring, another year. It seemed to the emperor that the title "Dies Invictus Natalis" was a fine title for the Lord Jesus. He was right, but all that happened from his choosing of that date was that paganism and Christianity merged their celebrations—not truly Christian nor wholly pagan.

In Luke's account we have a very definite clue about the time of year. He mentions that there were "shepherds abiding in the fields. . . ." In the Judean hill country it is still custom to keep the flocks out on the ranges until bad weather sets in. That period is usually from the middle of March until the middle of October. Bethlehem is 2,500 feet above sea level, and by the middle or end of October the cold rains and winds begin, sometimes with snow flurries. When the weather gets too cold for the flocks and shepherds, they are brought in nearer to town into stone-walled sheepfolds built in front of the great limestone caves that honeycomb all those hills. Because the shepherds were still out camping overnight in the pastures, we know that the nativity occurred sometime between those dates of March and October.

John's Hint

In John's Gospel, although he does not give an account of the birth as such, since he is writing the story of God incarnate who has no beginning, he does give us an interesting hint about the time. John simply says in the first fourteen verses of his prologue that the One who was God became man, and then he adds: "He was *tabernacled* among us." That is the Greek word that is translated "dwelt." But the choice of the word is highly significant.

In the Old Testament the God of Israel had dwelt in the midst of His people in a Holy Tent or Tabernacle. Now He was to be "tabernacled" among them in a body of flesh. The Feast of Tabernacles is the first week in October. We really do not know what time of year Jesus was born, but it did strike me that John's use of that word might have been an oblique reference to the Feast of Tabernacles as the beginning of God's "tabernacling" with us in a body of flesh and blood.

The Morning Star

But to say what time of day? Impossible! Here I will add a personal conviction that I cannot prove by history and may not positively prove by Scripture; there are hints of something, however, and it is magnificent and important, not to be overlooked. I think that the Christ child was born in the early morning, just before daybreak, while the double morning star was shining. This was the same star that the Wise Ones were watching from their tower five hundred miles east in Sippar. The shepherds' cave had to be on the east side of the hill where Bethlehem sits—the shepherds' fields are east of town. In that case the cave opened toward the east and looked out on the Judean wilderness and the morning sky.

I think Mary also was watching that star through her hour of travail, for Zacharias had called her baby-to-be "the Day Star." Later, the Scriptures three more times refer to the Lord as the "Bright and Morning Star."

His first coming was as silent and beautiful as the morning star. Only those who were watching for Him knew He had arrived. "How silently, how silently, the wondrous Gift is given." The rest of the world slept on undisturbed.

When He comes to earth again, it will be as the "Sun of Righteousness," as visible, as inescapable as sunrise.

PART THREE
The Sky-Watchers

Star-Gazers in Sippar

Sunrise always seems so majestic and deliberate, but daybreak races across the face of the world at 1,040 miles per hour, lighting the mountaintops, sliding down into the valleys, sweeping away the stars. This is why on a certain morning during the reign of Caesar Augustus daybreak came to watchers at the Tower of Sippar in Babylonia at least forty minutes before it came to the hills of Judea.

The Observatory

In the "Land of the Two Rivers" about forty-five miles north of Babylon at the point where the Euphrates and Tigris come closest together (now in Iraq) there was an ancient university town called Sippar. For at least 1200 years, possibly 1500 years before Christ, there had been an astronomical observatory there. For all that time a daily record had been kept of the movements of the sun and moon, and particularly of the Wanderers, the planets that can be seen to move against the background of the "fixed stars."

Every night a group of men kept careful watch, and they knew many things. They knew, for instance, that the planet Venus has phases like the moon, and waxes and wanes. This can barely be detected, and only by the best eyes in the rarest kind of conditions. They also knew (and this is even more puzzling) that Saturn has rings. Their official picture of Saturn shows a god standing in a tilted ring like a tire around his waist.[1] Modern astronomers have always assumed that the rings could not be seen with the unaided eye—modern astronomy did not dream of such an arrangement on Venus until telescopes were invented.

These men of Sippar were the equivalent of our modern astrophysicists, and were held in similar esteem by their contemporaries. As Martinus A. Beek explains

> In one field where religion, philosophy and science meet there is no doubt about our dependence on ancient Mesopotamia, and that [field] is astronomy, motivated by astrology. Although the course of the stars as originally observed [was] for the sole purpose of foretelling the future, observation in the schools of Erech, *Sippar,* Babylon and Borsippa freed itself from this restriction and became scientific research in the modern sense.
>
> One of the most celebrated astronomers was Kidinnu of *Sippar* . . . he knew the difference between the sidereal year . . . and the tropical year, . . . [he] discovered precession, which is the motion of the equinoxes, . . . [and] was able to predict solar and lunar eclipses accurately."[2]

Jewish Astronomers

Since the time that Nebuchadnezzar took Jerusalem and transplanted many of the Jews to Babylon and its environs, many thousands had continued to live there. Even in New

Testament days there was a large colony of Jews in Babylon. Because many Jews excelled in the mathematical sciences, and gravitated to the related fields, it seems reasonable to assume that many of them studied in the astronomy schools of Sippar. There they would have cherished in captivity the statement from Numbers 24:17 that "there shall come a Star out of Jacob, and a Sceptre shall rise out of Israel." That, alone, was enough to give hope that there would be a great Jewish king, announced by a new star.

In Daniel 2:48 we read that Daniel was made the head of the four colleges of Babylon, which included the schools of astronomy. That could account for the wise men having a tradition that Saturn was the "Protector of the Jews" and that the zodiac sign of Pisces had to do with events in the land of Palestine.

There is another source of information on these long-ago events: the great Isaac Abarbanel (also spelled Abravanel), contemporary of Christopher Colombus and Vasco da Gama, treasurer of King Ferdinand and Queen Isabella, financial genius, philosopher, Bible expositor, and writer. He was born in Lisbon in 1437, and although he was forced four times in his life to flee persecution, he was always in the lands of his exiles the friend and advisor to kings and princes.

Abarbanel was a firm believer in the coming of the Messiah and wrote four books on that subject alone. He was vitally interested in astronomy and astrology and left an account of "certain Jewish astrologers who were regarded as wise men and who studied in a school at Sippar, Babylonia." He also mentioned that the ancient astronomers had predicted that the Messiah would be born when Jupiter and Saturn were in conjunction in the sign of Pisces. Because he had rejected the claims of Jesus of Nazareth (he lived through the terrors of the Inquisition that was carried out in that Name), he was unaware of the fact that such a sign had indeed accompanied the birth of the Lord Jesus Christ.[3]

When sputnik was first rocketed into orbit in October, 1957, the sleepy, chilly people who climbed out of bed to see it learned the first rule of astronomy. In order to find something among the stars one must know *what* he is looking for, and *when* to watch, and *where*. This is true of the Christmas star. We must know what object we are looking for, and what year it shone, and where.

Something Strange

On that certain morning we are considering, the men on the ziggurat were more numerous than usual because something unusual was happening in the sky. According to our calendar, it was in May, 7 B.C., that Jupiter and Saturn, the two largest planets (called "the Wanderers"), had come within one degree of each other just before daybreak in the eastern sky. On October 5 that same year the two planets came together again, this time at midnight, directly overhead. And now, for the third time, on December 1, they were once more in conjunction, this time southwestward in the sunset sky. This triple conjunction only occurs once in 805 years, and this time it had some added features that were highly significant to the astronomer-astrologers.

The conjunction was occurring in the zodiacal sign of Picses, the constellation of the Mediterranean lands. Jupiter indicated that the formation concerned a king—a very great king. Saturn was the protecting star of Israel. It could mean only one thing: a great king had been born to the people of Israel in Palestine on the Mediterranean coast.

It is still the custom, when an unusual configuration is seen in the sky, for astronomers to arrange an expedition to observe it. This the Babylonians did, and if they started out soon after the second occurrence in October, they would easily have reached Jerusalem by the first of December at the caravan rate of twenty miles a day.

It took many centuries of archaeology, history, and astronomy to put the pieces together and remember what the wise men had seen. Through the centuries from the birth of Christ until about the beginning of the twentieth century most of the Bible expositors wrote of the star of Bethlehem as though it were a great mystery.

There is an old French tapestry that shows the wise men as three richly dressed nobles on horses, following a ball of fire rolling along the road just ahead of them. A writer of the Reformation period offered the opinion, "It was a speciale fierie Ball travelling through the sky above their heads, but not a star."

Astronomers have considered the possibilities that the star of Bethlehem was either a supernova (an exploding star), or a comet; in ancient times these were thought to coincide with great human events. There was a comet over Rome just after Caesar's assassination—a very bad omen. No other celestial phenonenon, such as a fireball or a meteor, is even remotely comparable to Matthew's description of the event.

There are still in existence very detailed Chinese records of the appearance of Halley's comet in 12 B.C., but that is too early to be identified with the star of Bethlehem. John William's authoritative "List of Comets," complied in 1971, lists comet #52 as visible for seventy days in the spring of 5 B.C. in the Near East, and comet #53, a comet "without a tail" (later astronomers have concluded that it was a nova) was visible for three months in 4 B.C. Evidently the astronomers of 7–4 B.C. had an interesting time of it.

The real difficulty with either a nova or a comet is that neither of these, by any stretch of the imagination, could be considered to have "gone before" a group of travelers.

Even so large an object as our sun or moon could not be said to "stand over" any specific town. Moreover, a comet or a nova would have been seen by everyone in Palestine if it were in the sky; but it is apparent from the text that neither Herod nor anyone else had noticed anything significant or different in the stars. It had to be something that only astronomers would notice, and something that would move across the sky only very slowly.

There are three reasons why the mystery of the Bethlehem star was not fathomed earlier. First, only Matthew's Gospel mentions it; there is no cross reference for more information. (In this connection we should notice also that it is only Matthew, the chronicler of the star, who uses the words, "then shall appear the sign of the Son of man in heaven" [24:30] when recording the prophecies about the second coming of the Lord.) Second, the traditional translation of the verbs as the simple past tense gave a distorted impression of what happened (see next chapter). And third, the astronomers were all looking in the wrong year for some strange event that would account for the phenomenon.

Kepler, the Royal Astronomer

The pieces of the puzzle began to fall into place in the year 1603. Johannes Kepler, Royal Mathematician and Astronomer of the Court of Prague, observed a conjunction of Saturn and Jupiter in the constellation of Pisces. It was to be visible in late December of that year and into January of 1604. Possibly because it was so near to Christmas, it suddenly occurred to Kepler that perhaps such a conjunction had been the star of Bethlehem.

His charts showed that this particular conjunction happened every 805 years. Twice 805 is 1610 years, and this subtracted from 1604 would be back to 6 B.C. Kepler also remembered that the Jewish rabbi and philosopher Abarbanel had written that the expected Messiah would be born when this exact conjunction occurred in the sign of Pisces. Kepler made a note of this in his books, but did nothing further to pursue the matter, possibly because he assumed that it was six years too early.

Modern Archaeology Is Born

In the nineteenth century, when Napoleon discovered the wonders of ancient Egypt, modern archaeology was born. The past began to be dug up and deciphered. Until then most of the recent civilizations regarded the monuments of the past simply as handy quarries for good cut stone. All of the marble facings on the great pyramids had been removed to use on later palaces for the caliphs. The bricks from Babylon built a dam at Mosul.

Before and after World War I both German and English teams of archaeologists began a systematic exploration of the Middle East. There, north of Babylon, they found Sippar and its vast store of cuneiform tablets describing, day by day for centuries, the motions of the stars. Literally tons of these were shipped to Germany in hardwood crates. There a professor, Herr Schnabel, one of the few men in the world that could read cuneiform, began the laborious work of deciphering.

One day in 1926 Schnabel came across the record of the conjunction of Jupiter and Saturn converging and separating four times in 7 and 6 B.C. He remembered Johannes Kepler's notation. By now it was known that Dionysus Exiguus had erred by about six years. It all came together at last.

Astonishment in Jerusalem

Nowhere do the Scriptures say that there were *three* wise men that came to Bethlehem from the east. It is highly unlikely that only three men would take such a trip. If there *were* only three astronomers (and there may have been a dozen), they would have had many servants, for these men, while not in any sense "kings" as the famous old carol would have it, were men of great importance. Moreover, they were transporting an exceedingly valuable cargo, and armed guards as well as servants would be necessary.

So it must have been quite a caravan that headed off northwest toward the headwaters of the Euphrates at Haran. There it turned off southwest again, following the fertile crescent and the trade routes, more than a thousand miles. Actually, the straight line that daybreak takes from Sippar to Judea is only five hundred miles, but it was across the empty quarter, and no one attempted passage that way. It is still a risky business to cross that desert, even with the best equipment, and the most recent maps still show no roads.

The Astronomical Expedition

When this caravan arrived in Roman Jerusalem, it would have been one of many. One of the reasons Jerusalem was so valuable to the ancient empires was its position astride the land bridge between Europe, Africa, and Asia. It was the stopover for many caravans. The procedure would have been for the caravan to locate an inn or khan with accommodations for the whole crowd and the pack animals or wagons they were traveling with. (The Scriptures mention no camels, by the way, but it is a reasonable guess that camels were used, although horses or onagers and wagons often were used for such long trips.) As soon as they were settled, they began to inquire of the local folk about the great king (Jupiter) born to the Jews (Saturn) in the land of Judea (Pisces).

> Now when Jesus was born in Bethlehem of Judea in the days of Herod the king, behold [this word always introduces an astonishing thing], there came wise men from the east to Jerusalem [Sippar is due east of Bethlehem], saying, Where is he that is born King of the Jews? [That is all they could deduce from the stars.] For we have seen his star in the east [the Greek means not just "east" but "sunrising"], and are come to worship him. When Herod heard these things [their arrival and extraordinary request were reported to Herod immediately], he was troubled, and all Jerusalem with him. Matthew 2:1–3.

There was no small stir that day in the city. Remember that this Herod was the murderous old man who lived in daily fear that someone would take his kingdom and throne away from him. You can imagine how he would react to such news. He was insane, but cunning still. He called in the scribes privately (he had no intention of letting them meet the delegation of astronomers) and inquired of them where the Hebrew Scriptures prophesied that their Messiah-King would be born. That was an easy one to answer. For five centuries it had plainly said in Micah:

And thou, Bethlehem in Judea, although you are a small town among the thousands of villages, nevertheless, out of you will come He whose goings-forth have been from eternity. He will be ruler over Israel. Micah 5:2 (paraphrased).

The Time and Place

So *that* was where: Bethlehem. Herod dismissed the scribes. He sent a messenger to the astronomers that he would grant them an interview. How did he, the king, explain to these men that he had known nothing about it? At any rate, he spent much time, probably with interpreters, trying to get an *exact* date for the appearance of the phenomenon that had sent them on their journey. It may have been nearly a year since the astronomers had begun their watch on the narrowing conjunction.

Please note that there was no star like a searchlight standing over Bethlehem. Herod had seen nothing, nor had anyone else in Palestine. Only astronomers realized that something special had happened in the sky. Herod's problem was further complicated by the fact that Persia (for that is what it was called then) had a different calendar than Israel and both would have to be reconciled to the Roman calendar.

In return for their information about the celestial message, Herod told them that the child was in Bethlehem, less than two leagues away (a league equals three miles; Bethlehem is five and one-half miles southwest of Jerusalem). After giving them the directions they needed, he added, "When you have found Him bring me word, that I may come and worship Him also." Herod had not the slightest doubt that there was such a child. What he told the wise men must be read in the light of what Josephus says about one facet of Herod's character. " . . . [Herod] prosecuted his very kindred and his friends, and punished them as if they were enemies; this wickedness he undertook out of a desire that he might himself alone be honored.''[1] Herod literally could not bear to hear anyone else praised, and he worshiped no god, and no man but himself.

After coming so far, the wise men decided that there was still time before dark to go such a little way. Finally, after all those months of uncertain anticipation, they would actually see the child. As they went out the south gate of Jerusalem, where the road drops away into a long winding valley southwest to Bethlehem, like all good astronomers they were watching the sunset sky. Suddenly, in the sunset glow, and apparently right over the town they were headed for, the saw the evening star. It was their conunction!

And not only their conjunction, but Saturn and Jupiter had been joined by Mars, making a great blazing triangle of light, for it was now February, 6 B.C. (The light is always referred to as ''*the* Star'' because it was Jupiter the King Star they were watching, as the other two moved close to signal the birth of the King.)

> And, lo, the star, which they saw in the east, went before them [westward], till it came and stood over where the young child was. When they saw the star, they rejoiced with exceeding great joy [its appearance this last small step of their journey verified what they had believed]. Matthew 2:9, 10.

It is obvious that if they had been following something all of the way, they would not have been so surprised and delighted to find it again.

The translators have a choice when translating the aorist Greek verb. They can say, ''The star that they *saw.* . . . *went* before them'' (simple past tense). Or, they can use the English pluperfect tense that describes action completed, not continuing, and say, ''The star that they *had seen* . . .

had gone before them.'' Because the King James translators had no clear idea of what the star might have been, they used the simple past tense, and that is what gave readers the idea that the wise men were following a moving light.

In less than an hour they could have been in Bethlehem, and now, there was no problem about where to find the child. Enrollment had been over for some months. The great crowds had gone home; all except Mary and Joseph who had decided that David's greater Son should be reared in David's town. They had rented or bought a house.

Now the word used for the child (in Matt. 2) is not the word used in the account of when the shepherds came on the night of His birth. Then it was *brephos,* the "newly born" (compare I Peter 2:2). Now it is *paidion,* "the little boy." Don't get your theology from Christmas cards. They were born out of the story tellers of the dark ages, who had little or no access to the Scriptures.

> Jupiter, Saturn, and Mars—
> gods to the ancients,
> gods to Greece and Rome.

> But they are not gods to God,
> who gave them light and motion
> and fixed their wandering course
> among His stars.

> He called them to assemble,
> saying,
> "I go to Bethlehem:
> Stand in the sunset sky
> and mark the town."

Journey's End

There was no problem in finding the child, for as we mentioned, the scandal of Nazareth had become the pride of

Bethlehem. Surely the whole town watched His growth with amazement and delight. After all, He was and still is the only perfect human being ever born, unmarred and unhandicapped by sin. Any child playing in the street could have told the caravan where to find the house of Joseph and Mary and the wonderful baby. Notice that the text plainly says "the house," and not the cave or manger.

> And when they were come into the house, they saw the young child with Mary his mother, and fell down, and worshipped him. Matthew 2:11.

What did He look like? Did God keep a baby book for us to see some day? It must have been quite a scene—the little house crowded with these distinguished visitors, and all of them on their knees in wonder and awe before the toddler. They didn't have to ask to see His birth certificate. They didn't have to verify that He was born when the double morning star shone over Bethlehem. When they saw Him, they knew that the whole trip had been worthwhile. Again, Mary listened quietly while they explained about seeing the stars come together, and she carefully put away in her treasure chest of memory every word. It was full of glowing jewels—and also now, the one like a heavy black stone that spoke of "a sword."

After much talk, and because it was now late, the astronomers went to the inn of Bethlehem that now had plenty of room. But their night's sleep was not to be very long. About midnight they woke up from nightmares they could hardly believe. It sounds as though more than one of them had the same dream sent by God, a terrible nightmare in which they saw Herod as he really was, trying to kill the young Prince.

Immediately, they got up, had the animals loaded, and the whole caravan started out by night. This was most unusual, but astronomers are not afraid of the dark. They made a wide circle to avoid Jerusalem, going up the coast road through Caesarea, and eastward across Galilee to the King's Highway.

> God knows, starlight is
> little enough to travel by.
> The prophecy was old and dim,
> the road unmarked.
> Nevertheless, in Bethlehem
> we found Him.
>
> Let every tinselled
> trivial package stir
> memories of gold,
> of frankincense,
> and myrrh.

Terror in Bethlehem

As soon as the astronomers were safely out of town, God sent another dream to Joseph. He saw Gabriel again, who said:

Gabriel's Sixth Message

Arise, and take the young child and his mother, and flee into Egypt, . . . for Herod will seek the young child to destroy him. Matthew 2:13.

Joseph was always instantly obedient to God. It is one of his many admirable traits and one that made him worthy of the great trust. He arose immediately, dressed, woke Mary, and together they packed only the most immediate necessities.

Wrapping the sleeping baby, they went quietly out of town before dawn. If anyone was sleepless that night in Bethlehem, and listening, they must have been puzzled about all the commotion in the small hours. When the sun arose that day, Joseph and Mary and the little Lord Jesus were well on their way to Beer-sheba and the Via Maris that goes to Egypt.

Did Mary hear from travelers about the terrible atrocity in Bethlehem? Her child was safe from Herod, but by now she must have known about all the other young mothers and their little ones. *All under two years old!* Herod had given his paranoia plenty of leeway. Maybe she thought then, "Is this the sword?" It would be more than thirty years before she understood just what the sword was.

Herod's Death

Within about a year, or at the most, two years, the angel of the Lord came to Joseph in a dream for the third time, this time to tell him that Herod was dead. Herod's death occurred during the Jewish Passover. There was an eclipse of the moon at the time, so it is possible to fix the date on our calendars as April 13, 4 B.C. Herod died a lingering death; he was horribly disfigured and in great agony. Shortly before his death, he commanded all the principal men to assemble and come to him. So urgent was this order that to refuse was to risk execution. Herod complained bitterly to Salome and her husband Alexis that the Jews had never been grateful to him for all the benefits he had bestowed upon them in rebuilding their temple, repairing the aqueducts, and the like. Also he was greatly distressed knowing, "I shall die without being lamented, and without such mourning as men usually expect at a king's death."

Such was his mental ability that even in his death throes he thought of a way to solve these problems. He ordered all the assembled principal men of the nation locked up in the hippodrome. When his death was announced, they were to be slaughtered. This would be his revenge against the Jewish people, and also provide a nationwide deep mourning at the time of his funeral. Fortunately, once he was dead, there was no madman with authority to carry out his demonic plan, and the men were released. Herod's body was taken with parades of great pomp and pageantry to the sepulchre he had prepared for himself, the mountain called "the Herodium," which is near (of all places) Bethlehem.[1]

> But when Herod was dead, behold, an angel of the Lord appeareth in a dream to Joseph [this is the third visit of Gabriel to Joseph in a dream] in Egypt, saying, Arise, and take the young child and his mother, and go into the land of Israel: for they are dead which sought the young child's life. Matthew 2:19, 20.

We assume it was not long after the flight of Mary and Joseph to Egypt, because Gabriel uses the same word for a very young child as he did in the previous warning. Again, Joseph immediately responded.

> And he arose, and took the young child and his mother, and came into the land of Israel. Matthew 2:21.

He headed straight home to the house in Bethlehem he had left. He had no intention of returning to Nazareth.

> But when he heard [while on the road] that Archelaus did reign in Judea . . . he was afraid to go thither. Matthew 2:22.

Joseph was afraid to go into Palestine at all, and was probably much distressed about where to go. He had good grounds for being afraid. Bethlehem was too close to Jerusalem for safety. Herod Archelaus was so harsh, in fact, that the Jewish rulers, who had put up with his father, sent a delegation all the way to Rome to ask to have him deposed. Rome obliged and then there was no king in Judea. So Rome then sent a series of procurators, that is, "Place Keepers," who simply held Judea for Rome for the next thirty-five years. That is how Rome became involved in the death of Bethlehem's Son of David the King.

Home to Nazareth

Nothwithstanding, being warned of God in a dream
[Joseph's fourth set of directions], he turned aside [from his
plan to return to Bethlehem] into the parts of Galilee; and he
came and dwelt in a city called Nazareth . . . Matthew 2:22,
23.

Once more the gossips down at the well had some big news.
Joseph, Mary, and the baby had come back to Nazareth.
"Well, whoever His father is, He certainly is a beautiful,
smart little boy."

And the child grew, and waxed strong in spirit, filled with
wisdom: and the grace of God was upon him. Luke 2:40.
And Jesus increased in wisdom and stature, and in favor
with God and man. Luke 2:52.

These two verses sum up the beautiful, silent years of
maturing in Nazareth.

> He had measured the heavens
> with a hand-span.
> He had weighed the oceans
> in the hollow of His hand,
> as a cook might measure
> a teaspoon of wine.
>
> He had molded in clay
> a perfect statue of Himself,
> and called it "Adam."
>
> Now the skillful hands would be
> working wood in Nazareth,
> shaping ox-yokes
> perfectly balanced, satin-smooth—
> "Take My yoke—it is easy, and light."

Genesis 2:7
Isaiah 40:12

A Number and a Word

The Number

A number of biologists, anthropologists, and statisticians have estimated that there have been about 12 billion people (including the present 4 billion inhabitants) who have lived on the planet earth. This figure was arrived at by using the rate of increase per generation, the scant records of written history, and information from archaeological finds which indicate the size and population of ancient cities. Surprisingly, this same approximate figure has been advanced by both evolutionists and by the creationists who base their calculations on the biblical family records and time spans.

The Word

The word *unique* means "the only one of its kind." In popular usage it is often qualified, such as: "very unique" or "quite unique," neither of which is possible. A thing either *is* or *is not* the only one of its kind. It is an absolute term that cannot be modified.

Whether the figure of 12 billion is anywhere near the true total of the human race, we have no way of knowing. But we do know that in all those 12,000,000,000 births, the birth of the Lord Jesus Christ *was unique*. The best proof that the record of the birth is true is the life that followed. There has never been through all the unreckoned ages before, or the two millenia since, among all those twelve billion births and lives, another like that one Man. He is the Unique Man and Immanuel—God with us.

Notes

Chapter 1

1. Flavius Josephus. *Antiquities of the Jews*. XVI:V:1.

Chapter 2

1. David L. Cooper, *Messiah: His Final Call to Israel*. (Los Angeles: Biblical Research Society, 1962), p. 11.

Chapter 8

1. Josephus. *Antiquities*. XVLI:VIII:2.

Chapter 9

1. Norton Wagner, *Unveiling the Universe*. (New York: Research Publishers, 1932).
2. Martinus A. Beek, *Atlas of Mesopotamia*. Trans. D. R. Welsh. (New York: Thomas Nelson and Sons, 1962), p. 147, my emphasis.
3. Paul Goodman, et al., *Isaac Abravanel: Six Lectures*. Ed. J. B. Trend, trans. H. Loewe, (Cambridge University Press, 1937), pp. 57–60.

Chapter 10

1. Josephus. *Antiquities*. XVI:V:4.

Chapter 11

1. Josephus. *Antiquities*. XVII:VI:5.

Bibliography

Beek, Martinus A., *Atlas of Mesopotamia*. Thomas Nelson and Sons, New York, 1962.

Durant, Will, *Caesar and Christ*. Simon and Schuster, New York, 1944.

Evans, I. O., *Discovering the Heavens*. Roy Publishers, New York.

Goodman, Paul, et al., *Isaac Abravanel: Six Lectures*. Cambridge University Press, 1937.

Gordon, Ernest, *Notes from a Layman's Greek Testament*. W. A. Wilde, Boston, 1941.

Griffith Observer. Vol. 39, no. 12, Griffith Observatory, Los Angeles, 1975.

International Standard Bible Encyclopedia. Eerdmans, Grand Rapids, 1960.

Josephus, Flavius. *Antiquities of the Jews*.

Keller, Werner, *The Bible As History*. Hodder and Stoughton, London, 1956.

Maier, Paul L., *First Christmas*. Harper and Row, New York, 1971.

National Geographic Society, *Everyday Life in Bible Times*. 1958.

Peloubet's Bible Dictionary. John C. Winston, Philadelphia, 1925.

Pictorial Bible Dictionary. Zondervan, Grand Rapids, 1963.

Scofield Reference Bible. Oxford University Press, New York, 1945.

Wagner, Norton, *Unveiling the Universe*. Research Publishers, New York, 1932.